XTREME ART

DRAW MINI MANGA!

CHRISTOPHER HART

WATSON-GUPTILL PUBLICATIONS/NEW YORK

INTRODUCTION

Welcome to the charming, mischievous, and funny world of mini manga characters, also known as *chibis* (pronounced CHEE-bees). *Manga* is the Japanese word for "comics," made famous by the big-eyed style of cartooning. And *chibi* is Japanese for "little." Chibis are the most adorable manga characters in the world, and they're irresistible to manga fans. Chibis are always getting into trouble! They just can't help it. They love having fun!

This book is filled with all sorts of silly and clever chibi characters for you to draw. Each drawing is broken down into four simple steps. Start by tracing or drawing step 1. Then add the red lines in steps 2, 3, and 4. It's easy! A few of the drawings have backgrounds, which you can either trace or draw if you like.

Professional cartoonists usually begin a drawing with large, basic shapes and then work in the details. By following the step-by-step drawings in this book, you'll be learning how to draw mini manga cartoons the way the pros do, without any trouble. Well, that's enough yapping—now let's get started!

Tips for Using This Book

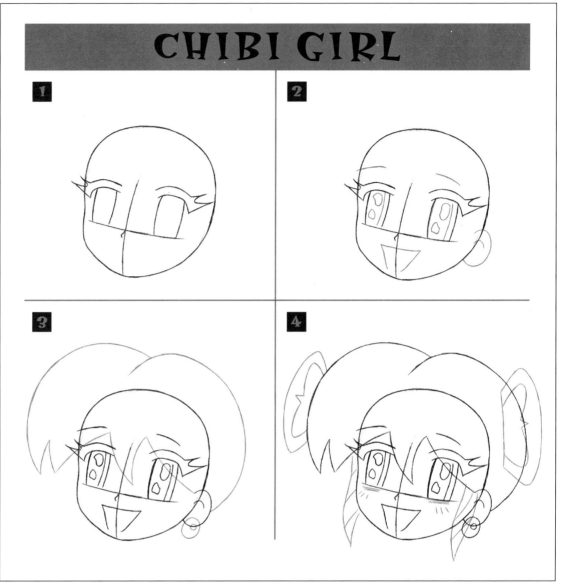

CHIBI GIRL

1
2
3
4

Trace or draw what you see in step 1. Then add the new lines (shown in red) in steps 2, 3, and 4. Draw with a light, sketchy line. Don't worry about getting it perfect on the first try.

When you've finished the steps, erase the guidelines (the criss-crosses) and any other lines you don't want to keep. Go over the other lines to make them darker.

Color it in, and you've got a clean, bold drawing!

THE BASICS

Here are some basic tips before we start drawing mini manga characters.

The chibi head is actually made up of a large circle and a small jaw. Sometimes it's easier to combine the circle and jaw into one basic head shape, which we will try later in the book. For now, we'll start with the basics.

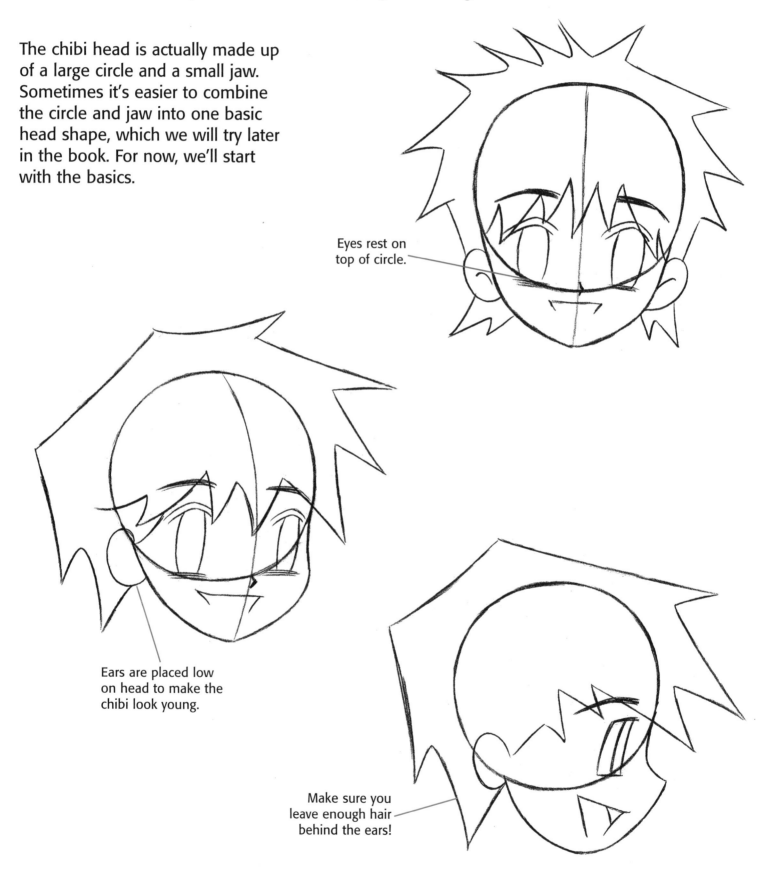

Eyes rest on top of circle.

Ears are placed low on head to make the chibi look young.

Make sure you leave enough hair behind the ears!

Cartoonists use three basic angles to draw the mini manga head. At each angle, the shape of the head changes a little bit.

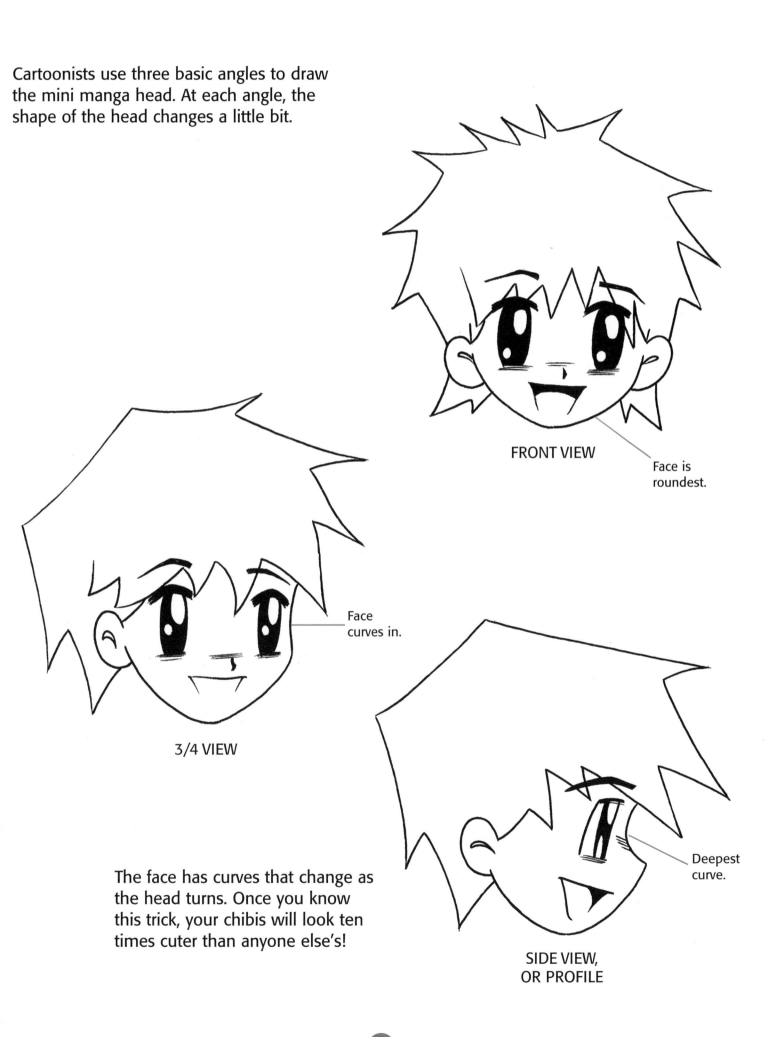

FRONT VIEW

Face is roundest.

Face curves in.

3/4 VIEW

Deepest curve.

SIDE VIEW, OR PROFILE

The face has curves that change as the head turns. Once you know this trick, your chibis will look ten times cuter than anyone else's!

When you draw the front view, don't draw the head as a complete circle. It looks old-fashioned. Instead, draw the face getting wider at the top. This gives the chibi more personality.

JUST OKAY

BETTER!

When you draw a 3/4 view, don't make the outline too round. Make sure the forehead curves in and the cheek bumps out.

JUST OKAY

BETTER!

Curves in!

Bumps out!

Here are three basic ways to draw eyes for playful and cuddly chibi characters.

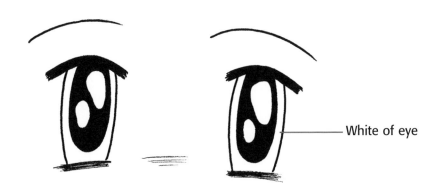

White of eye

Enclosed Eyes
An outline is drawn around the eyeball.

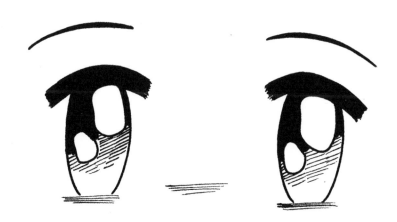

Shaded Eyes
Note the thick eyelids.

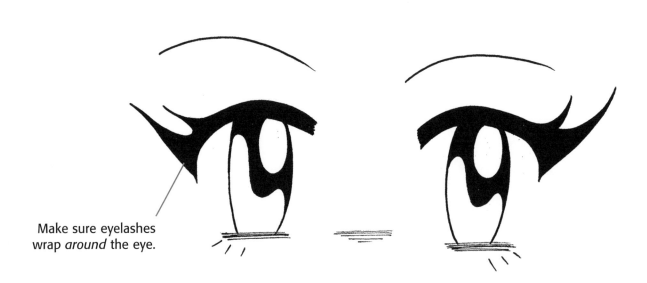

Make sure eyelashes wrap *around* the eye.

Girl's Eyes
Girls get big, glamorous eyelashes.

If you look at a baby's or a toddler's face, you'll notice that the younger the person is, the lower the eyes are on the head. Chibi eyes are always placed low down on the face.

Mini manga mouths should be simple. Try not to show too many individual teeth or make it too detailed. Sometimes manga artists even leave part of the lower lip blank to make a drawing look more stylish. Try it!

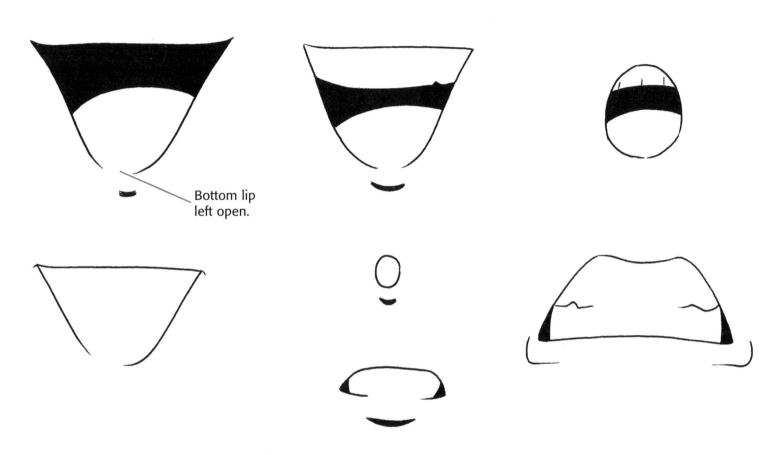

Bottom lip left open.

Let's practice some good hand positions. When drawing chibi hands, keep them simple—like mittens. You can even leave out the fingers if you want to. Here are three ways to draw the chibi-style hand. See which way you like most.

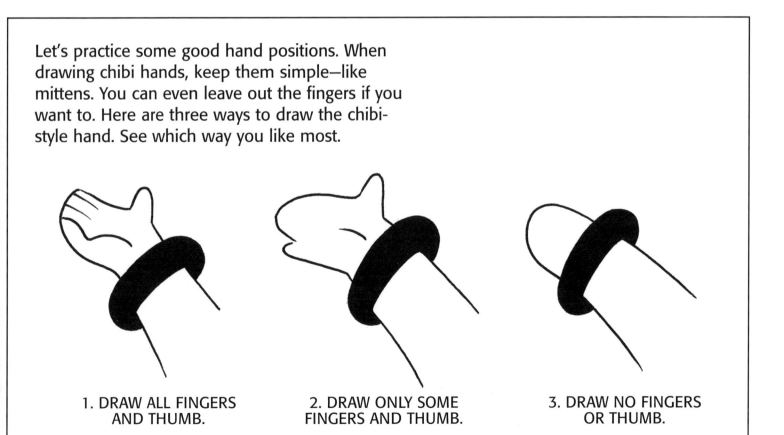

1. DRAW ALL FINGERS AND THUMB.

2. DRAW ONLY SOME FINGERS AND THUMB.

3. DRAW NO FINGERS OR THUMB.

When drawing hair, the rule is: more is better, and much more is best! Manga hair is wild and big. The only mistake you can make is not drawing enough of it.

Boys tend to have pointy hairstyles, with the points all combed to one side.

TOO LITTLE HAIR

MUCH BETTER!

Girls have hair that is flowing and graceful. They can have ponytails that go down to their knees!

LOOKING GOOD!

NOT ENOUGH HAIR

You can also add big jewelry. Remember this hint: little people take big jewelry.

HERE'S ANOTHER HINT: MINI MANGA CHARACTERS HAVE NO NECKS. A NECK WOULD MAKE THEM LOOK MORE GROWN-UP, INSTEAD OF LIKE SILLY CHIBIS!

When the neck shows, the character looks a little bit older.

When there's no neck, he looks younger.

NOW TURN THE PAGE AND START DRAWING MINI MANGA!

NUTS FOR NUTS!

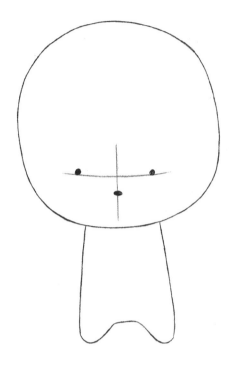

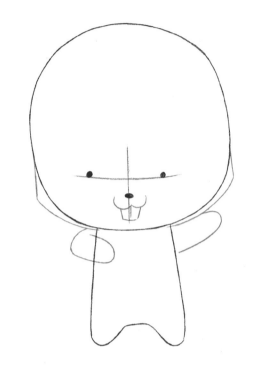

BO-BO THE BINKSTER

1

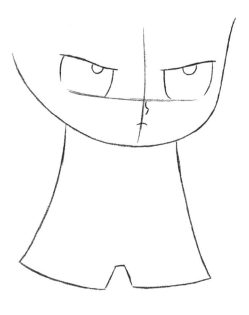

2

3

4

SLUGGER SARAH

1

2

3

4

1

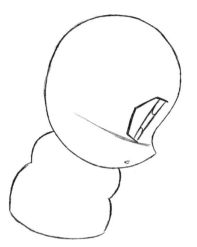

2

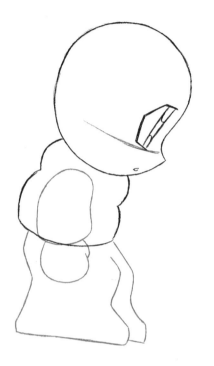

3

4

SHADOW MONSTER

1

2

3

4

TRICK OR TREAT!

SEASICK SAM

1

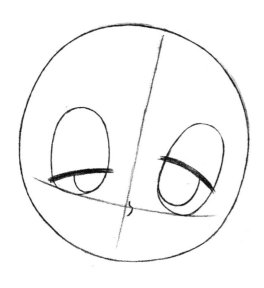

2

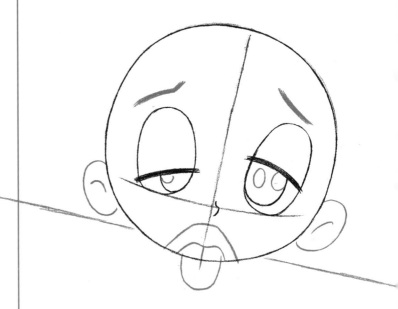

3

4

MINI MONSTER

1

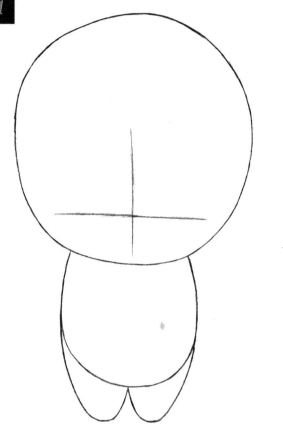

2

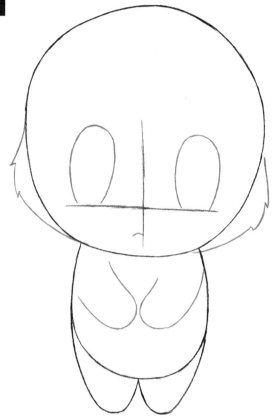

3

4

MIDNIGHT FAIRIE

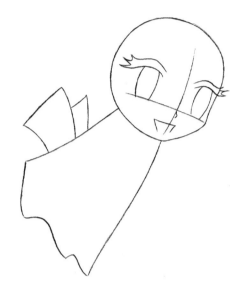

1

2

3

4

VOLTS AND JOLTS

1

2

3

4

GLITZY GIRL

1
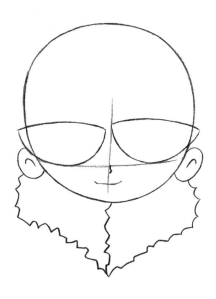

2

3

4

1

2

3

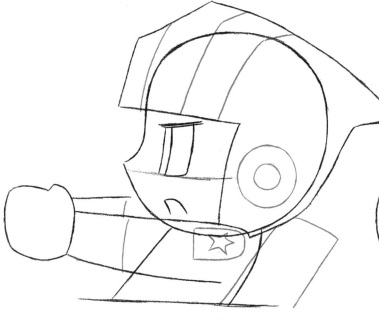

4

TINY TROOPER

1

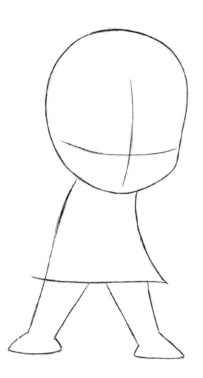

2

3

4

1

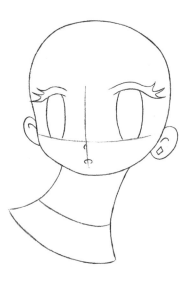

2

3

4

COACH CRUNCH

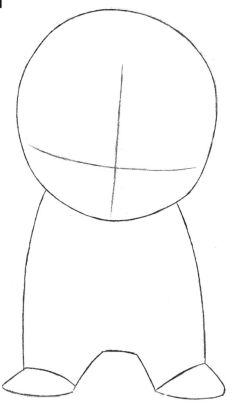

LUMPY LESTER

1

2

3

4

DON'T TAKE MY PUPPY

1

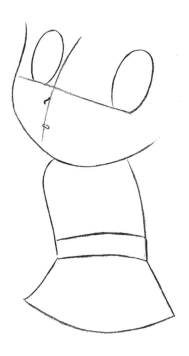

2

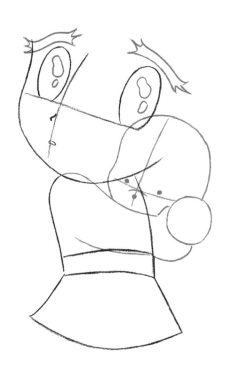

3

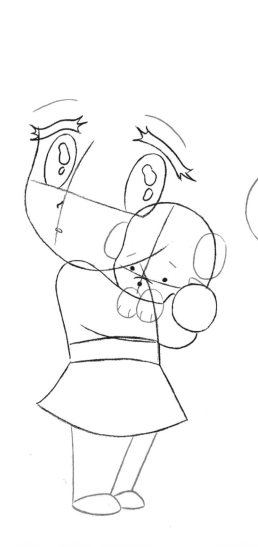

4

KARATE CHUNK

1

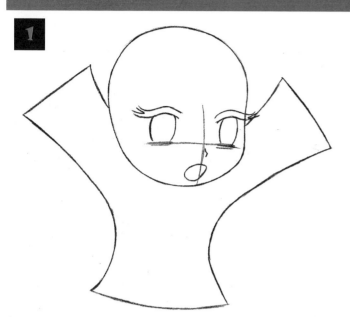

2

3

4

1

2

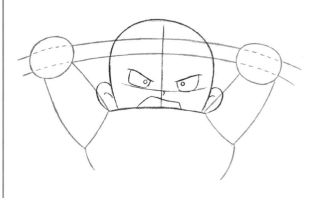

3

4

1

2

3

4

1

2

3

4

PILOT BOY

1

2

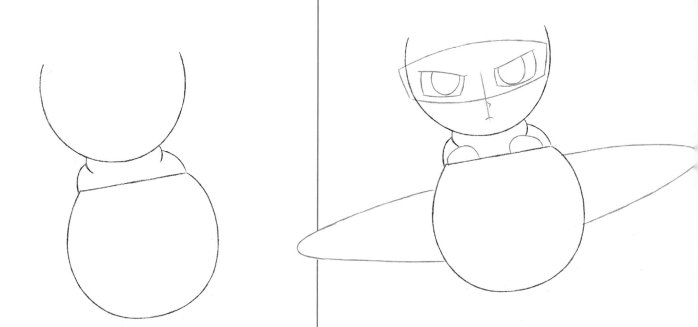

3

4

FASHION TEEN

1

2

3

4

WEE KNIGHT

1

2

3

4

1

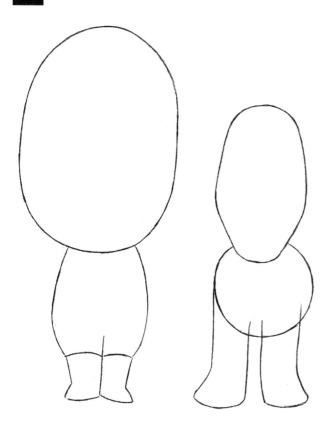

2

3

4

Senior Acquisitions Editor: Julie Mazur
Editor: Amy Dorta
Designer: Bob Fillie, Graphiti Design, Inc.
Production Manager: Hector Campbell
Text set in 13-pt Formata Regular

All drawings by Christopher Hart.

Cover art by Christopher Hart.

First published in 2006 by
Watson-Guptill Publications,
a division of VNU Business Media, Inc.
770 Broadway, New York, NY 10003
www.watsonguptill.com

Library of Congress Control Number: 2005930130

Printed in China

First printing, 2006

2 3 4 5 6 7 8 / 13 12 11 10 09 08 07 06